FOUNDATIONS OF A PROFITABLE BUSINESS FROM HOME

*Launch Your Business Step by Step
and Earn Income Faster!*

DR. TINA FRIZZELL-JENKINS, PCC

Foundations of a Profitable Business From Home:

Launch Your Business
Step by Step and Earn Income Faster!

Original Copyright ©2016 by Just Traders International, LLC
ISBN: 9798589498738

Published by: Just Traders International, LLC

Editors: Alan Jay Prescott and Willis S. Jenkins, Jr.

Cover design and illustration: Tina Frizzell-Jenkins/Nada Orlic

Interior design and production: Alan Jay Prescott

Printed in the USA

Updated: December 2020

Disclaimer: This book is intended to provide accurate information in regards to the subject matter covered. All information in the book is deemed accurate; however, the author and publisher take no responsibility for any legal actions incurred due to the contents of the book. The reader is advised to consult expert professional guidance as required for individual and business circumstances.

All rights reserved under International Copyright Law. No part of this book may be reproduced in any form (except for the inclusion of brief quotations in review), stored in a retrieval system, or transmitted in any form by any means—electronic, mechanical, photocopy, recording or otherwise—without prior written express permission of Tina Frizzell-Jenkins and Just Traders International, LLC.

*Dedicated to the memory of Dad,
Tillman Frizzell, Jr., and
to the strength of Mom,
Aretha S. Frizzell*

Table of Contents

Acknowledgments 1

Note from the Author 2

Foreword 3

Chapter One: Make the Switch 6

Chapter Two: Niche Selection 16

Chapter Three: Entity Protection 34

Chapter Four: Business Planning on Purpose 45

Chapter Five: Business Finance 58

Chapter Six: Business Image 68

Chapter Seven: Business Marketing 79

Chapter Eight: Tax-Smart Documentation 95

Chapter Nine: Income Techniques 108

Chapter Ten: Meditation 111

Tina's Thank You Bonuses 114

About the Author 115

Invite Dr. Tina Frizzell-Jenkins To Speak At Your Next Event 118

Bonus Chapter: Intellectual Property: Your Hidden Treasure ... 119

Resources 128

Acknowledgments

I acknowledge my Lord & Savior Jesus Christ for being my foundation, my guide and my strength, and for my prayer partners.

I acknowledge my husband and best friend, Willis, for being my helpmate and my rock, and for the three "T's," Tinille, Tenise and Trent, who keep me current.

I acknowledge my extended family for their untiring support of my endeavors. I can always count on their encouragement.

I acknowledge the students of my work who have made the decision to be continuous learners and to take action to fulfill their purpose.

I acknowledge every helping hand with this project from the editing, to researching content, and to the design.

—Tina Frizzell-Jenkins

Note from the Author

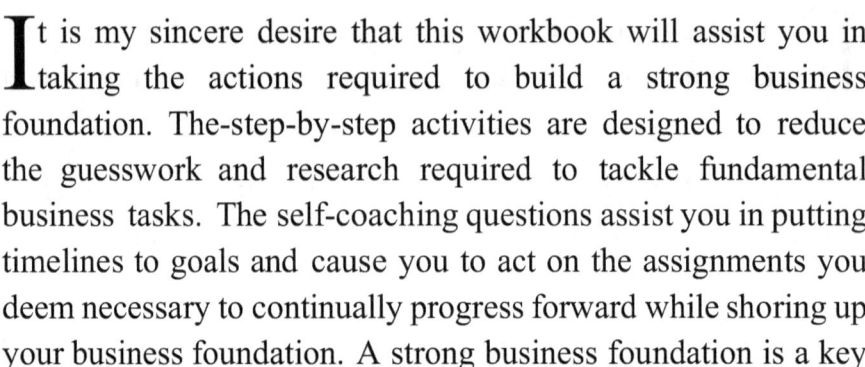

It is my sincere desire that this workbook will assist you in taking the actions required to build a strong business foundation. The-step-by-step activities are designed to reduce the guesswork and research required to tackle fundamental business tasks. The self-coaching questions assist you in putting timelines to goals and cause you to act on the assignments you deem necessary to continually progress forward while shoring up your business foundation. A strong business foundation is a key to a lasting business life.

Congratulations on taking action!

Foreword

Ask anyone who knows me well and they will tell you that I have never wanted to start a business. As a matter of fact, I spent the first 20 years of my marriage convincing my husband that he should never start one either. I always thought that it was wiser and safer to be an employee and let someone else be the boss and have all the worries. So how did a nice girl like me wind up starting and operating two separate businesses?

Well, starting my own business was borne out of necessity and not any burning passion that I felt the need to quench. It was not something that I had dreamed of all my life. In truth I had financial obligations, a new baby, medical issues and a constant battle between my employment and my need to have greater control over my own life and time. With that as impetus, I began the daunting trial and error process of becoming a business owner with my first home-based business back in 1978. As you can imagine, trial and error is rarely the desired course of efficiency. How I wish I could have had a step-by-step guide as to what I would need to succeed written in simple easy to understand terms.

Fast forward to now and "Thank you" Tina for writing this book. No one interested in starting a home-based business should ever go it alone and now they don't need to. Tina Frizzell-Jenkins is my cousin by marriage and I was so pleased to connect with her again after many years only to find out that she was a successful business owner herself. This book is a quick read and designed to answer questions that you may not even know that you need to ask.

Tina's common sense, layman's terms approach starts with assisting you to get your mind right, then proceed in a thoughtful way. Each chapter ends with self-coaching questions to help you think deeply about the process and self-check. The fundamentals are all there from how to write a business plan to accounting essentials. Tina's background as an empowerment coach helps her use the value of questions and self-talk to help you crystallize your vision.

She fully intends that you use this book as a workbook that serves both as a guide as to next steps and a journal of accomplishments or contemporaneous thoughts.

And speaking of home-based businesses, don't just think small potatoes, some of the most successful businesses in the nation started in someone's home or at least their garage. If you don't believe me then think of names like Google, Apple, Microsoft, Amazon and Disney, you get the picture.

As with many things in life the simplest answers are typically the best and this is no exception. With so many opportunities available, rarely has there been a better time to start building your own business. And, as with any building, a solid foundation is the key to stability. So, much success to all of you entrepreneurs as you embark on what could be the next big thing!

Carolyn E. Howell

Founder, Owner & CEO Events USA, LLC

Chapter One

Make the Switch

Make the switch from a "one day/someday" mentality to a "today" mentality relative to starting a business from home or building one you've already started.

I hear someone saying, "The timing's not right."

I say, "Get real." As with most things in life, the timing will likely never be *right*.

Make the Switch: change your mentality today. Change your legacy for tomorrow.

Use an acrostic for the word SWITCH to align your thoughts and principles of working a business. Notice I said *working a business* and not *being in business*. In order to have a vibrant business you have to take action, be intentional, be specific, and be consistent.

Let's get started.

S is for SIMPLY.

Simply decide to do the business of your choice. The business you start with doesn't have to be the business you end up with. I promise you the principles you learn and the mishaps you overcome will be the stepping stones in the success of future business ventures. You'll be so much smarter.

"Do" is the action word. Starting a business can be tedious and hard work, especially if you're starting from scratch. How- ever, turnkey businesses work best for a lot of folks because as the name implies, most of the startup work is done for you. Direct sales and referral marketing businesses fall in this category. These kinds of businesses also afford you great opportunities to learn business principles and offer huge time savings. For example, if you start a home-based business that's turnkey, you're likely to get the website as part of the deal. Whereas in a self-starting new venture, the website setup will cost you time and/or money.

W is for WAITING.

Waiting is no longer an option if you're serious about your financial future.

Start small if you must, but *start*.

From the beginning, make it a habit of implementing good business practices. Make your business legal, establish good accounting and tax practices, and make integrity a priority in those you partner with to do business.

I is for I RESIST THE ORDINARY.

"I resist ordinariness and mediocrity" gives you the guts you re- quire to look at a naysayer and declare, "I was meant for prosperity. Forgive me, but I approached you because I thought you were, too."

T is for TRUST.

Trust that you have what it takes to be successful and what you don't you have the good sense to find.

Mentors can help with guidance and with what you don't know or haven't been exposed to.

Borrow my belief in you. I believe you have the ability to be successful by taking the necessary steps to launch the business of your choice from Point Zero to out-of-this- world success.

C is for CEO.

You're the captain of your ship...embrace the title. Build an enterprise you can get excited about and be proud of.

H is for HIS FAVOR AND YOUR FAITH.

Call those things that be not as though they were! Speak your success daily and expect great success daily.

Need a coach to simplify the process and get result faster, check out Coach Tina FJ.

My confession goes like this:

I Declare...

"I'm blessed. I'm prosperous. I'm healthy and strong. I'm physically fit and the weight I should be. I have much favor. No weapon formed against me shall prosper. I'm intuitive. I'm a confident woman of God, confident coach, confident seminar speaker and confident business owner. I'm the head and not the tail. I'm the lender and not the borrower. I'm stress-free. I'm a servant leader and a giver. I'm the daughter of the King." Amen.

Write *your* confession:

I Declare...

_____

_____

_____

_____

_____

Most folks who know me personally know I like to give things away. Write 7 statements of confession and email them to me at iresistordinary@tinafrizzell.com. In return I'm going to email you a link for a FREE download.

The rest will be up to you: Make the Switch.

Go from not speaking your declaration every day to speaking your declaration every day. Make the Switch and expect results.

Speaking of results, one could say Walt Disney had success.

Did you know he started in his garage? He started several businesses and lost almost every cent at one time, yet he never gave up.

How about you?

Walt was serious about leaving a legacy and he took serious measures.

What if he'd called his enterprise "John-John's Place" or "Cool Walt's Hood?" What if the main email address was littlewd@yahoo.com?

Customers, banks, lending institutions and vendors might not have taken the establishment seriously. That's what I see with a number of home-based businesses: poor structural decisions from the beginning. Much like your own name, your business name is something that should have meaning and character, and you should be proud of it.

Make the Switch.

Make the switch from a weak business foundation to a strong one.

Your business name is the start of your business structure. If you can't think of anything that has a specific meaning around the business you choose, use your own name and add "Enterprise." There are several Fortune 500 companies that are So and So Enterprise. The important thing is that you appear serious.

Your email address also speaks to who you are.

Can I suggest that you make an effort to purchase your own name or your initials and your last name? This nomenclature can follow you no matter what business venture you choose to pursue.

Make the Switch.

Promote yourself first and the company with which you are associated next. Promote yourself as the awesome entrepreneur who happens to choose to market a particular product or service.

You are an independent marketing representative for the majority of the direct sales or referral marketing business. So tell me, why do you take on that company's identity and shed your own? I submit that you're not as serious about your business as you could be because you hide under the spotlight of their business instead of blending its spotlight with yours to create a much richer product or service because you are the content provider. The customer doesn't just get the product or service but the customer gets *you*. You make the exchange of products and services enjoyable and comfortable. Repeat customers buy the experience.

Make the Switch.

Going forward, ensure your customers know they're not just getting a product or a service but they're getting you.

Before you purchase another business card with the name of the company you represent on it, make sure you have your own business card branding you professionally and creatively first.

Let's review:

We talked about Making the Switch from a someday mentality to a today mentality relative to getting your business established and launched.

We used an acrostic for the word SWITCH that gave us some principles for thinking like the entrepreneur we strive to be, followed by a declaration of success.

We talked about establishing a business name and email that will be strong components in the structure and foundation of your business.

Lastly, we talked about branding your business so it reflects *you*.

Ask yourself, "Will I make the switch so that 3 days, 3 months and definitely 3 years from now I'll be glad I did?"

Or will you pull these notes out 3 years from now and ask, "Where would I have been if I'd just taken action?"

Make the Switch. You deserve it. Start today.

MAKE THE SWITCH Self-Coaching Questions What am I passionate about?

How can my passion create profits? Where do I see the most favor in my life? Where do others notice favor in my life?

Write down seven things that come to mind as you reflect on answering the above questions:

1. _____

_____

_____

_____

_____

_____

2.

3.

4.

5. _____
_____
_____
_____
_____
_____

6. _____
_____
_____
_____
_____
_____

7. _____
_____
_____
_____
_____
_____

Elaborate on the top 2 thoughts from above and how what you are passionate about can produce profit or intertwine with the business opportunity you are considering:

1. _____

_____

_____

_____

_____

_____

_____

2. _____

_____

_____

_____

_____

_____

_____

What can you agree to pursue on a regular and consistent basis with the intent to earn a profit?

_____

_____

_____

_____

Chapter Two
Niche Selection

What is a niche? I'm glad you asked. *Webster* has a couple of definitions, as follows:

The situation in which a business's products or services can succeed by being sold to a particular kind or group of people (generally a smaller, more targeted subset of a particular market);

and A recess in a wall, especially for a statue.

Obviously, from a business perspective the first definition is the one that appeals to a business situation. However, let's consider the second definition to put a visual image to the first definition.

Picture the niche you choose being so special and unique that it's elevated to statue status and placed in a carved-out section of the wall for display.

SELECT A GOOD NICHE

Focusing on a specific niche (as opposed to a broader market), you have the opportunity to be the online expert or authority in that niche. This will help you grow a loyal customer base. Also, your niche differentiates you from the larger superstore-type websites that sell to the bigger market but don't have the niche expertise that online buyers like.

What makes a good niche?

There are several factors that make some niches better than others, such as products with a high profit margin, low competition online and high demand. Generally, the better job you do at choosing your niche, the more money your business will make. Later we'll visit a technique to determine the potential profitability of your niche.

In addition to wanting a profitable niche, you'll also want to think about the following:

How many people within your niche are willing to spend money?

How often will people within this niche willingly buy products repeatedly?

How many new people will be looking for products within your niche on a regular basis?

How many available suppliers are there for the products within this niche and how available are they to you?

What is the likelihood that your niche will allow you to hit your financial goals?

How can you pick a niche if you don't have one? Consider brainstorming.

BRAINSTORMING TECHNIQUE FOR PICKING A NICHE

What is brainstorming?

Brainstorming, according to *Webster,* is a technique that involves the spontaneous contribution of ideas. Use a flipboard to capture your ideas.

Brainstorming Rules

- No idea is a bad idea; therefore, write all of them on your flipboard
- Combine like ideas to be sorted later
- The focus is on quantity and not quality
- Consider "out of the box" ideas without judgment
- List 125 to 150 ideas
- Use a timer (optional)
- Make it a group activity (optional)

Niche Triggering Ideas to Brainstorm

- What interests you?
- What are your hobbies?
- What do associates, friends and family tell you that you do well?
- What skills do you have?
- What blogs interest you?
- What trade magazines do you read online or have a subscription to?
- What goal do you have?
- What type of volunteer work gets you excited?
- What club would you join?
- What would you do without being compensated?
- What would you stay up all night to do if you knew the out-come would pay you well?

NARROW YOUR NICHE

Once you choose your niche, make every effort to narrow it to a micro niche. This is the niche within the niche that allows you a better opportunity to be an expert and to build a loyal customer base.

IMPORTANT: YOUR NICHE SHOULD CONSIST OF THREE OR MORE WORDS to be used for Google purposes later in this exercise.

Examples:

If your niche is selling windows, you may want to sell storm windows or triple-glass windows or windows for office buildings as your micro niche.

If your niche is dentistry, then your micro niche might be traveling dentistry.

More examples:

Market	Niche	Micro Niche
Shoes	Ladies' Dress Shoes	4-Inch Stilettos
Golf	Driver Golf Club	Left-Hand Driver Golf Club
Travel	Family Vacation Resorts	All-Inclusive Family Resorts

Practice Chart:

Market	Niche	Micro Niche

Brainstorming Worksheet

1. _____
2. _____
3. _____
4. _____
5. _____
6. _____
7. _____

8. _____
9. _____
10. _____
11. _____
12. _____
13. _____
14. _____
15. _____
16. _____
17. _____
18. _____
19. _____
20. _____
21. _____
22. _____
23. _____
24. _____
25. _____
26. _____
27. _____

28. _____
29. _____
30. _____
31. _____
32. _____
33. _____
34. _____
35. _____
36. _____
37. _____
38. _____
39. _____
40. _____
41. _____
42. _____
43. _____
44. _____
45. _____
46. _____
47. _____

48. _____
49. _____
50. _____
51. _____
52. _____
53. _____
54. _____
55. _____
56. _____
57. _____
58. _____
59. _____
60. _____
61. _____
62. _____
63. _____
64. _____
65. _____
66. _____
67. _____

68. _____
69. _____
70. _____
71. _____
72. _____
73. _____
74. _____
75. _____
76. _____
77. _____
78. _____
79. _____
80. _____
81. _____
82. _____
83. _____
84. _____
85. _____
86. _____
87. _____

88. _____
89. _____
90. _____
91. _____
92. _____
93. _____
94. _____
95. _____
96. _____
97. _____
98. _____
99. _____
100. _____
101. _____
102. _____
103. _____
104. _____
105. _____
106. _____
107. _____

108. _____
109. _____
110. _____
111. _____
112. _____
113. _____
114. _____
115. _____
116. _____
117. _____
118. _____
119. _____
120. _____
121. _____
122. _____
123. _____
124. _____
125. _____
126. _____
127. _____

128. _____
129. _____
130. _____
131. _____
132. _____
133. _____
134. _____
135. _____
136. _____
137. _____
138. _____
139. _____
140. _____
141. _____
142. _____
143. _____
144. _____
145. _____
146. _____
147. _____

148. _____

149. _____

150. _____

151. _____

152. _____

153. _____

154. _____

155. _____

RESEARCHING YOUR NICHE

It's important to remember that you want to sell to the market what the market wants to buy. Be flexible with your niche. Don't fall into the trap of marketing products or services that only you and a few other folks are excited to purchase. You want hundreds or thousands of folks excited.

This is where the research comes into play. You want to be asking yourself a number of questions, such as:

How much confidence do I have that my potential customers will want to spend money on my product or service?

How much confidence do I have that they will repeatedly spend money on my product or service?

How much confidence do I have that there will be consistent new potential customers who'll want to spend money?

How much confidence do I have that there's a demand for my product or service?

How much profit is available?

How much do I have to earn to meet my financial goals?

What type of buyer do I expect (seniors, teenagers, business owners, middle class, upper class, impulsive, repetitive, careful, college students, new moms, parents, etc.)?

What other products or services can I offer the customer to increase the profit margin and add value to the customer's shopping experience?

Your research via the Web using Google will help you get answers to your questions. The bottom line is: Will the niche be profitable, will there be a demand and how can you successfully compete with your competitors?

RESEARCH TOOL

Google is a great FREE tool that is at your disposal to research your niche. Millions or perhaps billions of people search the Internet daily. How can you tap into this wealth of information?

The first step is to get an Adwords account. The Adwords account will assist you in analyzing your niche brainstorming ideas. A good niche has 3,000 to 10,000 searches per month. The com- petition will be high if there are over 10,000 searches per month. With searches fewer than 3,000 searches per month, the niche's traffic volume will likely not be profitable or yield sales volume.

Sign up for your Adwords account. Remember to use niche ideas containing at least 3 key words, because Google searches generally contain at least 3 words. Another important metric is the "commercial intention." The commercial intention signifies whether the person doing the search is doing it for research purposes or to make a purchase. The Ad Planner in your Adwords ac- count provides this useful information.

Sign up for your Adwords account now.

You'll be prompted for a business email address and your business website address. Click "I'm an experienced Adwords user" and bypass the email/website step to use the tool.

- Enter a username and password Select/click:
- "Tools and analysis"
- "Keyword planner"
- "Keyword and adgroup ideas"

- "Enter one or more of the following"
- "Get ideas"

Note: Set your target settings to US, English, Google, search partner, and negative keywords. Also click on "keyword ideas" and not "adgroup ideas."

In conjunction with the Adwords planner, download the SEO-quake.com toolbar (will not work with Internet Explorer) which assists you in discovering what page rank a website has. Google assigns a Page Rank (PR) to every webpage on the Web. The ranking is from n/a to 10, the former being the lowest and the latter the most difficult to achieve.

Start using your niche ideas in Adwords, remembering to keep them to 3 words or more. Look at the top 5 results for each niche and check for a PR under 3. If *all* the page rankings are 2 or under, then the competition is *good* for the niche idea. Otherwise, you know this niche is one that visitors don't frequent enough to warrant your pursuing as a business.

Contact a coach today to get clarity on your niche, Schedule Coach Tina FJ.

My first choice for a niche is:

_____

Second choice:

_____

Third choice:

_____

I've chosen this niche because:

_____

_____

_____

_____

_____

I've chosen these backup niches because:

_____

_____

_____

_____

_____

NICHE SELECTION Self-Coaching Questions

To what date do I commit in starting my niche brainstorming exercise?

_____

Who will participate with me in completing the brainstorming exercise?

_____

_____

_____

_____

To what date do I commit in finishing my niche brainstorming exercise?

_____

To what date do I commit in obtaining my niche Adwords account?

_____

To what date do I commit in completing the Adwords exercise?

_____

Chapter Three

Entity Protection

The answer to the question can be discovered by understanding the different possible structures of a business entity

But first, what exactly is an entity?

According to *Webster*, an entity is a business or organization that has an identity separate from those of its members.

You might ask, "Why do I want my business identity separate from the members of the business?"

If your business should fail or find itself in court for some reason and the business gets sued, then your personal finances and belongings will be used to meet the debt. A financial mishap in your business could ruin your personal finances or, worse, your personal life. Bad business breaks have a way of destroying relationships and causing life to spiral out of control. Though most entrepreneurs go on to have other successful businesses, some of the relationships are lost forever. Let's strive to avoid that scenario.

ENTITY: To Be or Not To Be?

The first business structure we'll explore is the Sole Proprietorship.

It is run by a single person (couples in some states) with the intent to earn a profit

The person owns all the business assets

Business and person are seen as one in the eyes of the law

The business pays higher taxes

The business/person is open to liability risk

When the business outgrows this structure, it must be dissolved and a corporation formed

Bank accounts have to be closed and new accounts opened with new legal name and documents; thus:

All tax credits are lost

Credibility based on former name is lost

Changes must be made to websites, business cards, etc.

Changes must be made to merchant accounts

The next structure we examine is a Partnership Business.

It is run by two or more people for the purpose of earning a profit

Generally, all partners bear personal liability

For tax reasons, all profits and losses are absorbed by all partners

There is no liability protection There are few tax benefits

Outgrowing the partnership model will have the same negative impacts as outlined above

The next structure we consider is a "C" Corporation.

It has its own identity, with a board of directors running it for the purpose of creating profits and possibly those of its shareholders

It has to be registered in and is regulated by the state in which it is doing business

It is responsible for employee taxes It is separated from the owners

There is very good liability/asset protection

Profits and losses do not flow down to the owners

There are multiple compensation choices, such as employee payments and dividends

Taxes are reduced

The fee is $500–$1,000 if one files the paperwork oneself in Maryland, for example.

The next structure we discuss is the "S" Corporation.

It has its own identity, with a board of directors with the purpose of earning a profit

It has to be registered in and is regulated by the state in which it is doing business

The business is separated from the owners There is very good liability/asset protection

There is generally no employee tax but there may be payroll taxes

The owner pays himself/herself a reasonable salary (what the owner would pay someone else), with or without a profit

If the business needs seed money the 'S' corp. is not likely a good choice.

The fee is $500–$1,000 if one files the paperwork oneself in Maryland, for example

Lastly, we'll take a look at the Limited Liability Corporation or LLC.

It has to be registered in and is regulated by the state in which it is doing business

It can be taxed either as a "pass-through" entity, like a sole proprietorship, partner- ship, or as a regular corporation. By default, an LLC is taxed as a pass-through entity, where the owners just pay taxes on the profits of the LLC at their individual tax rates.

By default, it is taxed as a sole proprietor if there is only one owner—which is why you can file business using an SSN instead of an EIN—or as a partnership if there is more than one owner.

The owner and a tax professional decide whether the business is more favorably taxed as an "S" or "C" corporation

The business is separated from the owners

There is very good personal liability protection against corporate suits

There is strong corporate asset protection against personal suits

The business is easier and more flexible to run than a corporation

An LLC enjoys the same tax benefits as corporation

All members can manage

The fee is about $200 if one files the paperwork oneself in Maryland, for example

Let's review:

We looked at five business entities' structures: sole proprietorship, partnerships, "C" and "S" corporations and LLCs.

Basically, we learned that the sole propriety and partnerships offer no liability or asset protection and that the 'C' and 'S' corporations offer the most liability/asset protection but are burdened by additional costs, taxes, fees and the increased administrative support required. Therefore, the business profit margin needs to be substantial for continued viability.

Therefore, three important aspects concerning choice of entity need to be considered:

- liability protection

- asset protection
- tax protection

The LLC appears the best choice for most home-based businesses, especially startups. It offers enough protection to keep the business identity separate from the members; thus, keeping the members' finances and assets safe from hostile takeovers. Plus. the initial startup and yearly operational expenses are much more reasonable for an LLC than a corporation.

The answer to the entity question "To Be or Not To Be," is "To Be!"

You definitely want your business to be an entity. Perhaps the true question is, "How long until your business is an entity?"

ENTITY PROTECTION Self-Coaching Questions

To what date can I commit to spending one hour to obtain the LLC application for my state?

_____

How will I complete the LLC application; or will I depend on a service?

http://www.legalzoom.com or google similar services.

_____

On a scale from 1–10 (with 10 being the most important), how important is it for me to initiate and complete the process of having my business become an LLC in the next ten days?

_____

_____

What fear that could potentially sabotage me from launching my business do I need to address simultaneously with taking my business to the next level? Who can coach me past that fear to keep me on track? (http://www.coachtinafj.com)

CREATE YOUR LLC

Grab a pencil and use the space allotted in this workbook, your computer, or tablet and follow along with the example below to start creating your LLC. Information required for an LLC for Maryland is as follows:

ARTICLES OF ORGANIZATION

The undersigned, with the intention of creating a Maryland Limited Liability Company, files the following Articles of Organization:

1. The name of the Limited Liability Company is:

   _____

2. The purpose for which the Limited Liability Company is filed is as follows:

   _____

   _____

3. The address of the Limited Liability Company in Maryland is:

   _____

_____

4. The resident agent of the Limited Liability Company in Maryland is

_____

_____

Whose address is:

_____

_____

5. Signature(s) of Authorized Person(s)

_____

_____

6. Resident Agent's signature

_____

7. Filing party's return address:

_____

_____

_____

Additional work space for LLC creation

INSTRUCTIONS FOR DRAFTING A LIMITED LIABILITY COMPANY

To create a Maryland Limited Liability Company (LLC), originally executed Articles of Organization must be submitted to:

Department of Assessments and Taxation

301 W. Preston Street

Baltimore, MD 21201-2392

1) Insert the name here.

_____

_____

The name must not be misleadingly similar to that of another LLC, Corporation, Trade Name, Limited Partnership or Limited Liability Partnership on file with the Department and the name of the LLC must include one of the following:

   a) Limited Liability Company
   b) L.L.C.
   c) LLC
   d) L.C.
   e) L C

2) Insert the purpose of the LLC. A one or two sentence description of the business is sufficient.

_____

3) Insert the address of the LLC. The address must be in Maryland and cannot be a P.O. box.

_____

_____

_____

4) Insert the name and address (cannot be a P.O. box) of the resident agent. A resident agent is another entity or individual designated to accept service of process for the LLC. The resident agent can be any Maryland citizen who is over eighteen, a Maryland corporation or a Maryland LLC. This person must also sign the document.

_____

_____

_____

5) Execution. Must be signed by any adult individual authorized by the persons forming the LLC.

_____

6) The resident agent must sign here.

_____

7) Insert the return address for any correspondence

regarding this filing.

_____

_____

_____

Note: This is a list of the mandatory provisions. Any provision the parties decide is relevant may be added to the Articles of Organization. Documents must be typed or printed. No handwritten documents will be accepted.

FEES (2017):

1) Certificate of Organization: $100

2) Certified copy of document above: $20 + $1 per page

3) Certificate of Status at time of filing: $20

Go to the following website for the online application for the State of Maryland:

https://dat.maryland.gov/Businesses/Pages/default1.aspx

Google: LLC requirements for your state to find a similar document.

Chapter Four

Business Planning on Purpose

What is a Business Plan? The following are a few definitions:

A written document describing the nature of the business, the sales and marketing strategy, the financial background, and a projected profit-and-loss statement:

http://www.entrepreneur.com/encyclopedia/business-plan

A detailed plan setting out the objectives of a business, the strategy and tactics planned to achieve them, and the expected profits, usually over a period of three to ten years

http://dictionary.reference.com/browse/business+plan

An essential part of your business's success and its ability to turn a profit is the business plan. This plan can be simple and yet insightful. It can also be used for tax purposes as a form of documentation of proof of the business's intent to earn a profit and for obtaining financial backing for the business.

The only way to do a business plan is to *do* a business plan. Get started by asking yourself a few questions and following the example provided. Be intentional and thoughtful as you use the template provided to document your business. The time and energy you put into this tool up front will save you time and energy in your business endeavors moving forward.

BUSINESS PLAN TEMPLATE

Below is a business plan template to use to start your journey. This is a plan that I purchased; however, it has been slightly altered. You can email me to obtain the author's contact information.

BUSINESS PLAN FOR:

(Company) dba Company—Medical One

LEGAL ENTITY:

Limited Liability Corporation

LOCATED AT:

Address:

CONTACT INFORMATION:

Telephone:

Fax:

Website: http://www.medicalone.com/

Email:

VISION STATEMENT:

Within the next five (5) years grow (Company) into a successful LLC earning $XX,XXX in the Maryland area Medical One independent distributor and recruiting company providing telemedicine services to Maryland blue collar workers.

COMPANY BACKGROUND:

Medical One website is www.medicalone.com

We are a 24-hour-a-day telemedicine company. Our members have unlimited access to our nationwide medical support team with a simple phone call. Licensed Physicians are available for all non-emergency medical concerns. When appropriate, and with sufficient information, our doctors may prescribe medication* 24 hours a day, 365 days a year. Medical One is available all day every day.

Name, Medical One Independent Representative (add your brief bio)

MISSION STATEMENT:

(Company), founded [your business start date], as a home-based business, intends to profitably mass market a growing number of products and services provided by Medical One to the general buying public. Due to low product prices, high retail profit mar- gins, large target audiences, and the tax incentives available to me by running this as a home-based business, I intend to produce a substantial profit over a period of time.

(Company) will provide high-quality products and services at the most favorable prices to my customers through personal sales, direct marketing, paid and or non-paid advertising, home-based product demonstrations, catalog sales, online promotion, fundraising support, etc.

PRODUCT / SERVICE DESCRIPTION

Telemedicine is the use of medical information exchanged from one site to another via electronic communications to improve a patient's clinical health statistics Telemedicine includes a growing variety of applications and services using two-way video, email, smart phones, wireless tools and other forms of telecommunications technology.

TARGET MARKET PROSPECTS

The target market prospects for my company's products and services fall into these general market categories:

- Male and/or female
- 21-50 years of age
- Households without medical, dental and/or vision services
- Employed/unemployed/underemployed

The prospects for my company's business opportunity are generally:

- Stay-at-home-mothers
- Small business owners
- Young adults aged 25–30 years
- Individuals without Social Security cards

CUSTOMER PROFILE

The ideal prospective customers are generally:

- Stay-at-home-mothers

- Small business owners
- Young adults aged 25–30 years
- Individuals without Social Security cards

The ideal prospective team members are generally:

- Stay-at-home-mothers
- Small business owners
- Young adults aged 25–30 years
- Individuals without Social Security cards

COMPETITIVE ENVIRONMENT

Bowie Urgent Care, which provides emergency health services. Their website is http://www.bowiemedicalcenter.com/

Oscar and Teledoc, which provide telemedicine medical services. Their websites are www.hioscar.com and www.teledoc.com respectfully.

CVS, which provides prescriptions. Their website is www.minuteclinic.com.

OUR MARKETING ADVANTAGE

(Company) will develop and deploy a marketing strategy that will aggressively promote Medical One premier products and services on a nationwide and international basis through retail customers, friends, relatives, business associates, and prospects generated through direct mail, websites, and other direct marketing activities capitalizing on the fact that we offer these three distinct benefits:

- One fee covers an entire family
- Medical services are available 24/7 with a certified physician

- Prescriptions are discounted up to 70%

OUR MARKETING STRATEGIES

In order to successfully sell against our competitors, I will market, advertise and promote my business on a consistent basis by:

- Community-located business card display
- Business introduction package ready for impromptu opportunities
- Attending and participating in a minimum of (number) of the community's business-to-business networking meetings per month
- Advertising at a local retail chain with an authorized advertising company
- Attending health fairs to market services
- Distributing 50–100 direct sales brochures per month

I will keep and maintain a computer and other necessary office equipment with adequate capabilities, storage, and speed to handle my business information and customer database.

I will maintain adequate business supplies such as order forms, recruiting brochures, and catalogs. I will have an adequate method of storing and transporting my business supplies to shows and demonstrations.

Positioning: Become nationally/locally known for my Afford- able Health Services

Revenue model: Generate revenues via telemedicine subscriptions as well as sales organization override

Initial Trial: Promote initial trial of products by a trial month of services

Client Retention: Retain clients by encouraging customers to use service within the first 30 days. Email current customers with relevant updates and medical tips.

Because of the broad appeal of the company's high-quality product lines, fair prices, and unique sales advantages, we will capitalize on the following sales strategies:

Direct Sales: Many of our retail customers with entrepreneurial potential will be converted to product distributors by simply showing them the advantages of owning their own business and how they can save by buying products at wholesale prices for personal use as well as profit from retail sales to their customer base.

Sampling: A small number of high-potential customers or distributors will be given products to sample. After a trial period, I will offer them an opportunity to become a preferred customer, to enjoy lower prices, or as a distributor, to earn income by telling others about the products.

Fundraising: I will provide *free* membership in my organization to any non-profit in order to help them establish, promote and con- duct a successful fundraising program. As a member, the organization may obtain products at wholesale prices to sell at retail. Our unique program for fundraising groups is to order gift certificates at 50% off retail for sale to the group at 25% discount.

Networking: Experts say that between 20 million and 25 million Americans are involved in network marketing today. Most are with companies that sell good-quality products. My company's fair prices and substantial advantages mean that these millions of experienced networkers are prime candidates for my business opportunity.

Direct Mail Advertising: In order to reach networkers, as well as tens of millions of other people interested in obtaining in-home medical services, I will consider conducting a direct mail marketing program as a part of my marketing efforts.

Classified Advertising: In order to reach the millions of potential retail buyers as well as potential independent distributors, I will explore the use of various forms of classified advertising to seek out prospects.

Word-of-Mouth: Since the most effective and most highly credible form of advertising is word-of-mouth advertising from satisfied customers, we will offer our current customers an opportunity to earn money referring new prospective customers to our company.

Media Exposure: Since it is possible to make the success of our company and the products we sell to appear "newsworthy" and to be of "human interests" we will attempt to entice local broadcast and print media to provide "free advertising" for our company and our products.

In-Home Meetings: Recognizing that the products and services provided by Medical One will be of benefit and of interest to the friends, family, contacts, former customers/clients, acquaintances, neighbors, colleagues, fellow civic club members, former employers and employees, vendors, suppliers, etc., in-home presentation meetings are planned as a part of my marketing effort.

Internet: We intend to aggressively utilize the Internet to present our message and showcase our product.

My daily plan as CEO of (Company) will be to promote the business, starting with a prospecting list or sales call as my first stop upon leaving my primary business location (home) every day, continuing if possible, throughout the day. Each evening, prior to returning to my primary business location, I will make a final prospecting call. This will include but not be limited to:

- Prospecting and making price comparisons at various merchant establishments rather than simply "shopping"
- Prospecting and promoting my company's products and services whenever playing golf, fishing or any other social or sporting activities conducive to business discussions
- Promoting my company's products and services at churches, schools, and numerous other appropriate activities

WEEKLY GOALS

- I will speak to at least one person about the business opportunity each day
- I will sell $50 in product in 3–5 days
- I will sell $150 in product each week
- I will sell to at least three customers each week
- My group will sell $400 in product each week
- I will conduct at least two presentations or parties each week

MONTHLY GOALS

- I will recruit two people each month
- I will speak to at least 20 people about the business opportunity each month
- I will sell $600 in product each month
- I will sell to at least 12 customers each month
- My group will sell at least $2,400 in product each month

ANNUAL GOALS

At the end of 20XX, I will have Y people in my sales force. They will generate $Z in annual sales, or an average of $Z per person.

I will personally generate $Z in sales. I will receive $Z in com- missions on my group's sales and $Z in commissions and income from my personal sales, for a total gross income of $Z.

My business costs (inventory, marketing, etc.) will be $Z. My net profit (loss) will be $Z.

LONG-TERM GOALS

At the end of 20XY, I will have 100 people in my sales organization. They will generate $240,000 in annual sales, or an average of $2,400 per person.

I will personally generate $15,000 in sales. I will receive

$24,000 per year in commissions on my group's sales and $4,950 per year in commissions and income from my personal sales, for a total gross income of $29,950.

My business costs (inventory, marketing, etc.) will be $5,000.

My net profit will be $25,000.

SUMMARY

(Company) will establish a track record of cost-effective products, excellent support and exemplary service to our customers. The products and services offered by (Company) and Medical One will continue to expand and diversify as we move forward.

Costs are likely to exceed income for an initial period, but (Company) intends to reach breakeven by the second year, and to generate steadily increasing profits thereafter.

Every business plan requires a financial report. A CPA can help you with this documentation. An example is below:

		Name/Description	S/U Amt	M2M
Title:		Profit & Loss / Cashflow Projection for "Your Business Name Here"		
Period:		January - December 2016		
INCOME				
	Source1	Personal sales commission	g	
	Source2	Team sales commission		
	Source3			
EXPENSE				
Telephone				
Advertising/Mktg				
	Internet	Internet access		50.00
	Newsletter	Advertising/promotion		199.00
	Other	Internet marketing fees		13.00
	Advertisement1	Marketing materials		99.00
	Advertisement2	Postage/mailing		
	Advertisement3	Printing		
	Advertisement4			
	Total Advertising/Marketing		0.00	361.00
Bank Charges				
	Merchant fees			
	Bank			
	Total Bank Charges		0.00	0.00
Meals & Entertainment				
Contract labor				
	Contract labor/purpose1			
	Contract labor/purpose2			
	Contract labor/purpose3			
	Contract labor/purpose4			
	Contract labor/purpose5			
	Contract labor/purpose6			
	Total Contract labor		0.00	0.00
Professional development				
	Professional development1			
	Professional development2			
	Professional development3			
	Professional development4			
	Professional development5			
	Professional development6			
	Total Professional development		0.00	0.00
Employee benefits				
	Name/type of employee benefits1			
	Name/type of employee benefits2			
	Name/type of employee benefits3			
	Name/type of employee benefits4			
	Name/type of employee benefits5			
	Name/type of employee benefits6			
	Total employee benefits		0.00	0.00
Rent/Lease				
Wages/Salaries				
	Business owner			
	Employee1			
	Employee2			
	Employee3			
	Employee4			
	Total Wages/Salaries		0.00	0.00

Business Plan Note Space

_____

_____

_____

_____

BUSINESS PLANNING ON PURPOSE Self-Coaching Questions

What is the deadline date I am setting to have this plan done?

_____

Who will create the plan?

_____

How many hours per day are needed for me to do the plan or follow-up to assure that the plan is done to meet the deadline?

_____

Who will be my accountability partner for this task?

_____

Chapter Five

Business Finance

Money is a tool. Most of you will agree with me that when you are performing a specific task or job, it will go a lot quicker and smoother with the appropriate tool.

Today, more than ever before, technology has made it possible for strangers to sneak in behind our financial closed doors and steal our money using *their* tools.

Not only do you have to be attentive and excited about accumulating your money, but you have to be vigilant in ensuring that financial predators stay away.

Here is a helpful acrostic for BUDGET.

BE WATCHFUL over personal and business finances. Oprah Winfrey said, "Sign all your checks." You hold on to that authority. Be an amateur accountant until you can hire a professional one. Accountants prepare and examine financial records, ensuring they are accurate and that taxes are paid properly and on time.

UNDERSTAND what is coming in and going out. You need to know what you actually have to work with. Understand the business cash flow. Determine on a monthly basis what the profits and expenses are. Create a simple spreadsheet to tally the numbers and give your- self a quick snapshot of the finances. This is part of the accounting but it is also part of the strategic business development. Strategy is required to alter your marketing structure or sales methodology.

DOUBLE CHECK your bank accounts by allotting one hour a month to quickly run through them to make sure they're in order. Record this task on your tax calendar. Checking your finances is a normal business function that can count as part of your regular and consistent business activities. This is the double check. The first check is actually looking at your credit card statements each month.

(I hear someone saying, "Checking my personal finances can count against my business time." The answer is yes if you are financing your home business using loans from your personal assets. Look at it this way. If you went to the bank to get a business loan the trip to the bank would be a deduction for mileage. The time you spend filling out the application would count as business administrative time. Well, you are your business's bank. The goal should be to have your business financially stable as soon as possible so that you're not using your personal finances.) Determine who will mentor you financially. Find someone successful in your niche if possible and someone outside of your niche to speak into your business life.

GET HELP if you need it. The small amount you pay for assistance could be a lot less than the amount you lose because no one is watching. Consider a small business accountant to start. Get credit for your business. Ask your banking institution for a debit card with the company name on it along with your name. After that, apply for a revolving credit card and ask for a small limit to start with, e.g. $500 or $5000. Set up automatic payments to assist in creating a pattern of paying regularly and timely. Did you know that with revolving business credit you are late after 60 days of nonpayment versus 30 days with personal credit?

EVERY good budget is in writing. Write the vision down and make it clear. The long-term business budget goal is included in the business plan.

TEST your spending habits. It's important to know when to suspend certain business habits that aren't working or just not getting the profitable results you want. You may occasionally have to reduce spending to keep the business in the black. Trustworthy partners are key. Find someone you can trust to assist you with money tools such as the ROTH IRAs and business credit. Get a trustworthy financial mentor, someone who can give you good advice and share pitfalls, too.

Who are you doing business with? How trustworthy and credible are your partners or business friends? Not every friend is a good business partner: most friends are best staying that way.

Consider friends' expertise before going into business with them.

Do they really have something tangible or intellectual to offer the business that can assist it in going to the next level? Or even maintaining the current level? Additionally, not everyone who has the expertise has the ethics, good work habits or solid reputation that should be contributed along with it. If all the friend has to offer is cash, then create a written agreement that makes him or her a silent partner. Be cautious. Beware of business buddies with undeveloped budgeting skills or have trouble with honesty.

Remember, your goal is to build a strong business foundation. Your wise choice of partners can increase the odds of prosperity. Poor choices may result in deterioration after starting to multiply the profits by breaking the partners' trust, undermining the integrity of the business, or selling business secrets for personal gain. List possible business partners:

Name:
_____

Justification:
_____

Name:
_____

Justification:
_____

Name:

_____

Justification:

_____

Things to remember in your business budget:

Website hosting fees Bank fees

Gas expenses Computer maintenance Training

Membership fees Merchant account fees

Labor with business activity (get help and pay fair wages) Remember all the business's expenses are tax deductions. Consult your tax strategist for assistance.

BUSINESS CREDIT

Incorporate the following 7 basic steps to obtain business credit:

1. The essential first step in building business credit is to separate yourself from your business by incorporating. Incorporate your business and get an Employer Identification Number (EIN). Remember, your EIN is to your business credit as your SSN is to your personal credit.

2. Use your business name, EIN and DUNS number to open a business checking account. Dun & Bradstreet are to your business's credit like the credit bureau is to your personal credit. The DUNS number is the most recognized and

widely used business identification number in the world, and obtaining one enables your business to start the process of building credit. It's often required for contracts with the United States Federal Government, state and local governments, and major retailers and is the global standard for business identification and tracking. Moreover, it can help prospective business partner's find you. Go to dnb.com to get your free business DUNS number and write it down here:

3. Simultaneous with opening your business checking account, open a business *savings* account with a $500 to $1000 deposit. If you don't have that much, put in what you can and then add 10% of your profits into the account with regularity, perhaps monthly. This habit helps to establish creditworthiness with your bank.

I commit to opening my business checking account within:

    2 weeks (actual date): _____

    3 weeks (actual date): _____

    4 weeks (actual date): _____

    5 weeks (actual date): _____

4. Take out a loan. Start small if you must but start. Request a $500 loan to purchase startup supplies, using the money in your business savings account as collateral. Set up automatic repayment and pay off the loan as soon as possible. Repeat the process, being careful to use the loan for business purposes only and repaying the debt timely.

I commit to getting my first business loan within:

    2 weeks (actual date): _____

3 weeks (actual date): _____

4 weeks (actual date): _____

5 weeks (actual date): _____

5. Apply for a business credit card using business credentials. Request a small limit and pay the balance off each month. After a few months you can request a limit increase. Repeat the process. Eventually, you'll apply for a business line of credit. Be patient: wait until business is producing regular profits and a pattern of sales has developed that can be easily noticed by the bank. Pay on time and in full.

I commit to applying for my business credit card within:

2 weeks (actual date): _____

3 weeks (actual date): _____

4 weeks (actual date): _____

5 weeks (actual date): _____

6. Obtain commercial credit by using your business credentials. Get the Internet, cell phone, utility bills, a Costco Club card, Office Depot/Staples and Vista Print business accounts for example. Pay on time and in full.

I commit to getting one form of commercial credit within:

2 weeks (actual date): _____

3 weeks (actual date): _____

4 weeks (actual date): _____

5 weeks (actual date): _____

7. Get trade financing, also known as business-to-business financing, a supplier will give credit to a business for 15–30 days. This type of short-term financing allows the business to establish a positive payment history. Your home business could offer clients bottled water when they visit, so setting up a bottled water account in the business name for six months is a great way to begin. Because personal consumption of any product relative to the business is not deductible, be fair and reasonable. If you get four containers of water per month and one is used for business, only deduct 25% of the bottled water bill.

I commit to getting trade financing within:

2 weeks (actual date): _____

3 weeks (actual date): _____

4 weeks (actual date): _____

5 weeks (actual date): _____

Over time and before you know it, you will have business credit just like you have personal credit. And they will be separate.

Let's review:

- Business structure is fundamental in obtaining business credit
- Getting commercial credit is an easy way to begin creating business credit
- Paying on time and in full ensures the continuation of your positive business credit standing

ACCEPTING PAYMENTS

You're in business to make money; collecting it for your services or products is paramount. You should take advantage of financial gateways that are quick, like PayPal, Cash App and Stripe. As soon as your income increases, you'll want to investigate a merchant account that's suited to your business goals.

1. Set up a PayPal account; go to http://paypal.com
   Click Signup

Click Business Select Standard Plan

PayPal Payments Standard

$0/month

Enter the email address you want associated with this account Add a password, your legal first and last name, legal business name, phone and address Select Agree and Continue.

Follow the instructions to activate your account.

Note: It's a good idea to link your PayPal account to your business checking account so you can move money between the two accounts seamlessly. Request your FREE card swipe right away.

2. Set up a Stripe account; go to https://stripe.com
   Enter your email

Confirm your email and Create a password

Agree to Stripe's Seller Agreement and E-Sign Consent.

Note: Signing up for Stripe is fast and free and there are no commitments or long-term contracts. You tell them about your business and there are no credit checks. They'll need some personal information to verify your identity. You'll be able to take payments and create a product price list.

3. Merchant Account

What are the advantages of a merchant account?

- With a merchant accounts you can usually expect the money paid by your customers to be deposited directly into your bank account within one to three days.
- With the monthly fee generally comes prompt and reliable customer service.
- Customers making a purchase stay on your website as op- posed to being sent to a third party to complete their financial transaction.
- The transaction fees may be lower.

4. Virtual Payments

- Cash App: Use your smart phone to send and receive payments.
- Zelle: Link your cell number to your business account to send and receive payments.

BUSINESS FINANCE Self-Coaching Questions

On a scale of 1–10 with 10 being the highest, how important is it to my business to be able to accept credit cards?

_____

To what date do I commit to setting up my Stripe account?

_____

To what date do I commit to setting up my Cash App account?

_____

Chapter Six

Business Image

Your business image has everything to do with how you dress your business. Ample thought has to go into the name of the business, the domain name you purchase, your logo, color scheme and business tagline.

BUSINESS NAME

Your business's name is personal; however, consider a name

that captures what is relevant to the business. You can use your "cell phone marketplace" to help you get a good understanding of what a sample market agrees or disagrees with relative to your business. This technique can be used to determine the best name or subtitle of a book, the best products to offer on a website, what title attracts a crowd for a seminar, etc.

Here is how the cell phone marketplace works. Come up with three names for your business or a book idea. Type a quick summary of the business or book. Text the summary and three titles to 20–25 numbers in your phone and notate how the marketplace responds. Use those data received to assist in determining the best name for the business or book for this example.

When choosing the name to text to from your cell phone marketplace, use contacts from different facets of your life, because you want an array of responses. If there are any contacts that fall in your niche of business, then you'll be particularly interested in their response.

List names of potential marketplace contacts that you can text to participate in your marketplace.

Brainstorming Worksheet

1. _____
2. _____
3. _____
4. _____
5. _____

6. _____
7. _____
8. _____
9. _____
10. _____
11. _____
12. _____
13. _____
14. _____
15. _____
16. _____
17. _____
18. _____
19. _____
20. _____
21. _____
22. _____
23. _____
24. _____
25. _____

List three business names (or other business components) that the marketplace can help you to determine:

1. _____

2. _____

3. _____

Domain Name

A domain name is a vanity address or an online calling card. Each website on the Internet has a physical address (your URL) and then a vanity name: www.yourdomainname.com

When choosing a domain name remember a few DOs and DON'Ts relative to purchasing domain names.

As a rule of thumb,

Do purchase memorable short phrases Do consider your niche

Do pick keywords if possible (e.g., if you are marketing markers, keywords might be *fine point, green, erasable*.)

Don't abbreviate

Don't buy premium/over-priced don't buy misspellings

Avoid numerals in your domain name (e.g., *success2day*)

After you settle on a domain name, test it in a marketplace. A marketplace can be a small group of business partners at your weekly business meeting. The contact marketplace list you created or a sampling from a snail mail campaign is an example. Have a few names for the marketplace to consider just in case your number one choice is not available.

The next step is to determine if your domain name choices are available. One source for getting domains is arbordomains.com. They're a little pricey but they get domains up and re-routed in minutes sometimes. Plus, they don't nickel-and-dime you for domain-related features like an e-mail address.

Choose a domain company that works for you and is dependable. I generally don't have hours or days to wait for my domain to be activated or change functionality, so I'd advise making a wise choice.

Predetermine where you're going to point your domain name if you don't have a website created especially for the domain name. When you purchase the domain name, you can point it where you want it to go at that time or at a later date. For example, tinafrizzell.com is not attached to a website so I can point it wherever I want and change pointing it as often as I want. I can't speak for other companies, but Hover allows me to complete this task almost effortlessly (https://hover.com/b4Nt8IK3).

Consider purchasing the domain name for 2–5 years if it's your company name, 1–2 years if testing a product or service.

If you didn't incorporate where to point the domain in the purchase process, you can add it after the fact by going to the menu in Arbor Domains and selecting Manage Your Account.

Input the domain name and password

Choose "DHS Host Entries, URL Redirection & E-mail Forwarding"

Click Web Forwarding Configuration Wizard

While you are there, decide whether you're going to cloak your domain name. (To cloak your domain name means to mask it. Wherever you point your domain, the HTTP site is what is going to show up in the URL unless you mask or cloak it to your nickname, your domain name.) Whether to cloak or not has to do with what you want the client visiting your site to see on the Web browser address line. It can be your vanity name or the actual address of the site. Note that some MLMs don't allow you to mask, so make sure you know their rules.

Let's review.

Your domain name is important because it's your calling card to your online clients. You want it to be short or an easy phrase to remember. Stick to .com, .net or .org and avoid misspelled words and actual numerals.

Use your credit card to purchase a domain name. Check the following domain names for availability:

1. _____
2. _____
3. _____

BUSINESS TAG LINE

A business tag line is a short phrase that is memorable and functional. That phrase generally is attached to the business or product name. Some examples are as follows:

State Farm: "Like a good neighbor, State Farm is there"

Coca Cola: "It's the real thing"

Bai: "Super fruit infused, antioxidant beverage"

Pork: "The other white meat"

When creating your tag line, consider the benefits. For example, when marketing ice cream, it can:

- Cool you down
- Leave you feeling refreshed
- Put a smile on your face
- Perk you up

Calling attention to the benefits is the key to better business sales online or in copy. If you have a website, you must be thinking about what's going to compel a new visitor to stay on your site. Visitors make quick decisions to stay or browse. You want them to stay, and your tag line can help visitors hang around to see what you have to offer.

List two topics or products and create 3 possible tag lines/benefits.

1. _____

   Tag lines/Benefits

   a. _____

   b. _____

   c. _____

2. _____

   Tag lines/Benefits

   a. _____

   b. _____

   c. _____

CUSTOMER SERVICE

Customer service according to the Web is "The process of ensuring customer satisfaction with a product or service before, during and after the sale. Often, customer service takes place while performing a transaction for the customer."

I like to say that customer service is not an office but an attitude. Remember, happy customers are usually return customers, and they tell their friends about you and encourage them to make purchases. The best form of advertising is word of mouth because it's cost-effective and it works.

Free works right? In reality, the advertising your happy customers are doing for you is not free. They are spreading the good word on your behalf because you've invested time with them. You know the cliché, time is money; you earned that advertisement with the awesome service you provided.

Let's talk a little bit about the client or the customer before we look at some customer service tips. Establishing a customer list is essential to the foundation of your business for three reasons.

1. A customer list helps to build your credibility with creditors. If you want a loan it is a plus to be able to show your bank that you have customers.

2. A customer list is the way to maintain followers of your business. That list can be helpful for a few things other than purchases, like business feedback, networking or referrals. For example, if you want to know how well your new website shows up for prospective new clients, ask your current clients to give you feedback on the new site.

3. If your business gets audited, the IRS auditor may try to disallow your deductions if you can't show a customer list or database.

- Your customer/client list needs to have more names than just family members, so be diligent in collecting client information.

- Consider a company to host your client database. That same company can provide several other services that are essential to communicating with your customers.

- It's a good idea to have a few customer lists. Sometimes breaking the list into categories is helpful as you expand your business services or products.

If you're like me when making a purchase online, you take a few minutes to read the comments. Often my purchases are made because of the comment, or the written word of mouth, if you will.

- Be intent on keeping your client or customer satisfied. Although every customer won't be agreeable, your job is to be honest, pleasant, informative and caring.

Now that we understand the importance of a customer list, let's go back to customer service by using an acrostic for CUSTOMER:

CLIENT. It is a must for customer service

UNIQUE. Every client is unique, so strive to cater to your clients' differences

SPECIAL. Treat your clients with care

TRUST. An important component in building client relationships

OPEN to flexibility in transactions. It's your business. Saving a client 20% today could net you several future sales

MEMORABLE. You want the client to have a memorable experience

ENTERTAINING. Make the buying experience fun (or pleasant at a minimum)

REPEAT. Repeat customers contribute to a growing business if you follow these tips, your client list will grow.

Let's Review

- You need clients to perfect customer service
- Customers are a key part of your business's strong foundation
- Customers are good for making purchases and helping to grow your business

Consult with the branding guru, Angelica Faith.

http://www.angelica-faith.com

BUSINESS IMAGE Self-Coaching Questions

What tag line will I vet through marketplace/business associates?

_____

_____

What color scheme will I be using consistently throughout my marketing materials?

_____

_____

To what dates do I commit to obtaining two domain names? (Your name [or variation of it] and a business name)

_____

_____

What customer service method resonated with me most? Why?

_____

_____

_____

_____

Chapter Seven

Business Marketing

Knowing Scheduling + Knowing Marketing = Knowing Profits

Marketing isn't just about sales; it's about building the kind of excitement around your products and/or services that transfers into referrals to their associates, friends and family. It's about staying on the minds of your clients. The following are a few marketing techniques that need to stay in your mind, especially in the beginning.

RELATIONSHIP MARKETING

Getting to know clients, what their businesses have to offer and what is important to them are key. Relationship marketing goes a long way when you remember a birthday, anniversary or special event with a card or note. Think of how you feel when your car dealer remembers your birthday.

NETWORK MARKETING

How do you show up at an event? Do you mingle with the intent of getting to know someone new or do you huddle in a corner waiting for someone to find you? Go with the intention of meeting and getting to know two or three new people.

More information: https://tinyurl.com/yy5unufh

E-MAIL MARKETING

Learn techniques to get the reader's attention, such as putting must-know information in the title of the message. Because your reader gets so many e-mails, be sure to make the title of the message catchy enough to grab attention. Think about what makes you open an e-mail when you have dozens to go through quickly.

WEBSITE MARKETING

An auto responder is a must-have tool if you're going to regularly communicate with those visiting your website. All of the names/customers/fans/followers you capture have to be catalogued so you can communicate with them.

I use a couple of Auto-Responder companies. Get Response is reasonably priced and integrates with several other platforms on the Web that you may use in the future.

http://www.paymetosocialize.com/

A Testimony from a fellow GetResponse user:

"I finally decided to fulfill my dreams and start my own company! Now I'm the proud owner of a small business offering a great product. Like many just starting out, I had a very limited marketing budget and was struggling to reach potential customers. I just couldn't generate enough sales to take my business to the next level. Then a good friend introduced me to a proven online marketing tool called Get Response that lets me email as many prospects as I can handle for a very reasonable price. It's true—I can create unlimited campaigns and follow-up messages, all for the same low price!

"I had read somewhere that email marketing is more effective than other, pricier tools, but I never dreamed I could learn to use it so quickly! Now I'm definitely not computer savvy, but in just 20 minutes, I had set up my first email marketing campaign and scheduled newsletters and follow-up messages for months ahead—all automatically. I didn't have to worry about looking professional either! GetResponse provides over 300 gorgeous templates so I'll never have to spend money for a graphic designer again (unless I want to!).

"After the first few campaigns, I began to realize that prospects wanted to see my products in action before making a purchase. Once again, GetResponse came to the rescue! With GetResponse Multimedia Studio, I can easily record and send high-impact video product demos with my messages, all with no added software or expense. The result has been awesome—response rates have doubled, even tripled! Customers feel like they know me and trust me and my products enough to buy them. And if tastes or budgets change, no worries! GetResponse lets me survey prospects and customers as often as I want to help me to stay ahead of the competition.

"The best part is you can try it for free— there's absolutely no risk. Don't let your concerns about cost or learning curves keep you from trying GetResponse. If you can email, you can use this amazing marketing service!" And don't you owe it to yourself to realize your full earnings potential? It's just a click away... http://www.paymetosocialize.com/

SOCIAL MEDIA MARKETING

Facebook, Twitter, Linked In, Instagram, Tiktok... These and more are absolutely necessary social media tools that require diligent attention. If you're working alone you may want to hire your children or somebody else to assist you with this marketing. Remember to pay market rates in order to assure the IRS that you are serious about your business.

If your marketing is not producing results you may be:

- Doing your marketing poorly
- Lacking in consistency
- Lacking in the ability to convey your superior expertise
- Failing to establish your reputation and/or credibility

To get more proficient at marketing on social media, the following pages provide some facts and tips.

FACEBOOK

Facts:

- The average user has 120–150 friends
- At least half of all users log on every day

- Only about 30% of active users live in the United States
- There are approximately 700 million users
- Billions of dollars are spent each month Tips:
- Set up a new account; it's a great way to separate your business from your personal life
- Create a fan page (fans are current or potential customers). You'll be able to share great content and promote special offers.

You can get personally connected with your target market. You can market on blogs and forums to get fans to join your fan page.

- The addition of a "like button" is a must because it gives your fans the opportunity to give you the "thumbs up." Thumbs up are great positive feedback—and the more you get, the more attention is paid to your post. The more attention to your post, the more opportunities you have to get a new client.

- Be a good content provider by regularly adding value to your page. Get the fans excited by posting hook statements that keep them checking back to your page. Increase the quality of your content and consider occasionally monetizing Facebook. If it's done occasionally, it'll seem natural.

- Create a vanity URL such as

  http://facebook.com/CoachTinaFJ.

- Consider worthwhile additions, such as contests, discounts, links to other sites, and starting groups with which your fans can interact.

- Make it a point to compliment your fans.

- Monetize Facebook by running ads that use the Pay Per click (PPC) system

- Automating Facebook will save you time and provide high value. YouTube videos and blogs can be posted to Facebook automatically.

- Boost visits to your page by using the Facebook feature "Promote," to get your targeted audience to your page.

Research/Google, "How to automatically post to Facebook" and add notes below:

_____

_____

_____

_____

_____

_____

_____

_____

_____

TWITTER

Twitter is the social media tool that helps you to create a following. Once people are following you, you can leverage the process to build strong relationships. This is another tool you can use to drive traffic to your website and ultimately get new clients.

Facts:

- Twitter was created in March 2006 by Jack Dorsey and launched in July of that year
- Twitter derives from the chirps birds make
- A mind-blowing 300 billion tweets have been sent since inception
- Tweets with image links have 5 times the engagement rate of those without
- China has the most users with over 35 million
- The average number of followers per Twitter user is 208
- Twitter only allows up to 140 characters per tweet Tips:
- Get followers and follow people who interest you
- Use the "favorite" feature to limit the information continually tweeted to you
- Follow 50 to 100 people per day
- Go to http://www.searc.twitter.com to get followers
- You want to stand out from the crowd by creating a customized background and providing contact information for your website, blog, and fan book page
- Tweet content that has value, that is interesting and exciting, something you would appreciate.
- Tweet ideas including a powerful question, articles, videos, blog posts, trivia, prize offers, the promotion of free services or products

- Google Twitter Automate to get a tool simply integrating twitter with your blog with your other social accounts. This will allow you to publish new blog posts that will automatically be tweeted to your followers. Use it to integrate feeds from other websites to publish automatically on your Twitter account. Use a blog you read that's run by someone else to publish content relevant to your niche and promote that content to your followers.
- #hashtags allows you to search for tweets that have a common topic or niche. For example, if you search on #COACH or #Coach or #coach, you'll get a list of tweets related to the Coach because the search is not case-sensitive. You'll get, "My coach had a birthday today" if "coach" isn't preceded by the hashtag.
- Loomly.com allows you to publish once across several social networks.
- Tools like buffer.com allows you to track the most popular tweets. It also provides analytics and helps to create social strategies.
- Hootsuite.com lets you schedule tweets on your time instead of having to schedule all future tweets in one sitting. After you have established yourself with worthy and interesting content you can begin monetizing on Twitter. Periodically, you can promote services and products. You can also drive traffic to your website for specials that your followers can only get by visiting your website or fan page. This is a great technique to in- crease the number of people associated with your website and/or fan page.

Set up your Twitter account by going to http://www.twitter.com.

When you sign up, you'll specify a name for the account, an e-mail address and a password. Have a logo or professional picture page and create a user name from your name. Choose the name if you like, or change it.

Follow the directions indicated and input the information above, click Enter and Twitter will display everything on the next page and create a user name from your name. Choose the name if you like, or change it.

Click create my Account and follow the prompts.

Twitter suggests that you start following five people and gives suggestions that you can accept. Initially, you want to follow a lot of people in hopes that they will in turn follow you.

Remember to adhere to your brand when creating the account: your account should match your website, fan page, e-mail, etc.

Continue through the process. You can add contacts from your e-mail address book or skip this step. Upload your image and the bio you've written.

While signed in to your Twitter account, go to http://www.dynamictweets.com.

Click the button to get started and proceed to the point where it asks you to add a Twitter account. Click the button to add it and the system will automatically start to link it with the dynamic tweets account.

Authorize Dynamic Tweets to use your account and follow the instructions to send out tweets in the intervals you prefer.

Fill in the boxes with a red *

Choose One Time or Recurring Tweets

Add content, the date and the time of the post and then click Post. Note that you can select the days you *do not* want to post.

Leave the schedule box blank if you want the post to continue indefinitely; otherwise put in a stop date.

Engage your audience by telling a story and asking powerful questions that lead up to an event or produce a sale.

Post to Twitter every three hours on general content and insert special event posts along the way. This method can achieve 500 or more followers within a few months legitimately without paying a service for leads.

Recycle Image allows you to re-tweet a tweet. You can only add a comment to the tweet if it is fewer than 140 characters. Other- wise you'll have to modify it to stay within the limit.

People like it when you re-tweet them. It shows you are thinking of them or paying attention to them, building a relationship in the process of obtaining a new follower. The more followers you have, the more potential customers to whom you can market your products and services.

Twitter (http://twitter.com/coachtinafj) has a YouTube channel (http://youtube.com/coachtinafj) that you can visit to learn more. There are other social media outlets that you can join like LinkedIn (http://linkedin.com/coachtinafj), Instagram (http://instagram.com/coachtinafj) and Tiktok to grow your network. Strive to keep your brand consistent for each business or product across the different social media platforms. Coke is the "real thing" in commercials, at the theater or on the Web. Take note of the marketing practices of successful products.

FACE-TO-FACE MARKETING

THE ELEVATOR SPEECH

You're now ready to market your business at networking events and will need to develop a story that conveys in a few minutes the reasons why the listener might want to hear more (The Elevator Speech). Commit to memory an elevator speech for potential clients that can pique their curiosity about your business or product.

Elevator Speech Examples:

For my home business—

"My name is Coach Tina FJ. I'm the Authority and Influence Coach. You know how folks struggle with increasing their influence and multiplying their message? I not only help them reduce the stress of building influence. I help them take action and make an impact thus increasing influence as they do what love and do it better"

"My name is Tina Frizzell-Jenkins. I'm an Executive and Leadership Coach. You know how folks struggle with the stress of work? I not only help them reduce stress, but I help them to take action to do what they love and do it better…. one conversation at a time."

My Elevator Speech:

_____

_____

_____

_____

_____

_____

_____

_____

_____

Test your elevator speech on a few worthy friends. Name

_____

_____

Constructive Feedback:

_____

_____

Name ._____

Constructive Feedback:

_____

_____

Name ._____

Constructive Feedback:

_____

_____

New Elevator Speech:

_____

_____

_____

_____

_____

_____

ONLINE MARKETING

FUNNELS

Funnels are the best marketing tool to use to sell your products or services. You can create the funnel that best suits your business goals, like a sales funnel, a product-launch funnel, an opt-in funnel, a membership funnel, or an automatic webinar funnel to name a few.

Funnels allow you to capture your customer's attention, tell your story and make an irresistible offer.

ClickFunnels provides an easy and complete solution for entrepreneurs like you to convert your products and services to cash without the hassle of learning code or hiring an expensive support team.

Get a two-week FREE ClickFunnels trial here:

https://tinyurl.com/ybd4juns

Get a FREE book/resource for successfully executing business online and for building funnels that convert to cash:

https://tinyurl.com/yx2sq27s

Also, want help creating content.

Free webclass, "How To Get ALL Of Your Sales Letters, Scripts And Webinar Slides, Emails And Ads Written (In As Little As 10 Minutes) WITHOUT Hiring An Expensive Copywriter!"

https://tinyurl.com/y95rof8w

BUUSSIINNEESSSS MARKETING Self-Coaching Questions

To what date do I commit to start creating my business's Facebook fan page? _____

How many hours a day, for the first week, will I spend creating my fan page? _____

What time-frame can I commit to in steadily reaching a goal of 25 fans?

Days_____ Week _____ Month _____

What is my vanity URL going to be called? http://www_____

How many days a week will I spend posting to my fan page? _____

(No fewer than 3 days if I am serious about my business and

using my fan page as a marketing tool)

How much money can I spend on PPC marketing on Facebook per week?

$ (this can be as little as $5)

After research on the Web, to what blog can I add quality content and the link to my fan page?

http://www_____

On what date will I upload my first video from my phone to my fan page? _____

What is the primary message I want my elevator speech to convey?

_____

_____

_____

What time-frame can I commit to in completing the first draft of my elevator speech?

Day's _____ Week _____ Month _____

What time-frame can I commit to in completing the elevator speech project?

Day's _____ Week _____ Month _____

To what date will I commit to start creating my business's Twitter account? _____

For how many hours a day, for the next week, do I commit to creating automatic tweets? _____

To what time frame can I commit to actively work steadily to until I reach the goal of 100 followers?

Day's _____ Week _____ Month _____

For how many days a week will I commit to focusing on retweeting until I get 100 followers? _____

(no fewer than 2 days if I'm serious about my business and using Twitter as a marketing tool)

Funnel Self-Coaching Question

What is the best funnel to use to increase your marketing results with your product or service?

_____

_____

_____

Chapter Eight

Tax-Smart Documentation

Documentation is essential to tax savings and to giving your tax professional the ammunition required to complete your tax forms accurately. There are three requirements for the tax success for those doing Business From Home: intent to earn a profit, documentation, and working the business regularly and consistently.

One way to document your regular and consistent business activities can be done with a calendar. Obtain a large, inexpensive calendar (hopefully before the new year starts!) that has enough blank area to make generous daily entries. Another solution is to print each month from a template in Word or to purchase a reasonably priced calendar program that you can use for several years going forward. If you use your phone or a computer for this, be sure to print the file each month and back up the files as you do for all your work. Electronics are great but they fail us sometimes. What- ever you decide, grab a calendar and get started now!

Create the calendar in advance of the month (on the 1st at the latest) to save a little time while creating a plan for the month, and use a pencil to make changes more easily. Add items to your calendar using the following examples as a guide.

April 7th is a Tuesday, so in the Tuesday block add Training/Personal Development at 8:30.

Most BFH are connected to a parent company that offers product calls, team-building calls and mentor calls, so add these regularly scheduled times and dates to your calendar. Use abbreviations and make a small legend in an empty box at the top or the bottom of the calendar.

Next add a time span weekly, bi-weekly or monthly that you'll spend providing customer service…calling clients to provide in- formation or solicit feedback.

Then add a daily time span (30 minutes to an hour) for checking and responding to your e-mails: prior to or after your day job; three days a week; or when you first arrive at your place of business. There are some advantages to this e-mail schedule that can be explored at a later date.

Add time for recruiting and expanding your professional

team, perhaps two to three hours every Saturday.

Make time twice a month to spend with a mentor. An IRS auditor will be interested in knowing you took time to increase your business knowledge from experts in the field.

Add other activities every month, such as marketing and sales of your product or services. Make the first day of the week Marketing Monday for one to two hours and customer sales three to five times a week.

Glancing at your calendar, you should see patterns of activities that increase your bottom line and show intent to make a profit.

The documentation of activities related to your Business

From Home (BFH) is a critical key to tax savings, so a few areas that are well worth your efforts are considered below.

Hire your minor children for age-appropriate work and pay them:

- Build funnels

  Customer retention activities

- Invoicing

Children earn and learn and the business gets the write-off... up to $12,000 to date.

List three task your children can do to assist the business:

1. _____
2. _____
3. _____

Business lunch or dinner is a popular choice when it comes to meeting with clients new or old. Within 48 hours of the event, write on the receipt. Deductions are allowed if the primary of the meal was discussing business.

- Purpose of the event
- Date
- Who was in attendance?
- Cost

Every BFH needs supplies and marketing materials and here are some typical examples that qualify as business expenses:

- Tablet
- Computer
- Cell phone
- Printer and cartridges
- Paper
- Marketing supplies, e.g. brochures, business cards, lawn signs, giveaways, domain names, hosting fees, seminars, membership sites, coaching, and publications.

List five supplies that are required for your business to be profitable below:

1. _____
2. _____
3. _____
4. _____
5. _____

If done correctly, a mileage log can represent significant tax savings, and it is a *must* if you want the actual or standard mileage deduction. Below are the elements that must be documented in the log:

- Primary purpose of the trip
- Date
- Total mileage (= odometer reading at end − odometer reading at start)
- Destination

Do a practice drive below:

Primary purpose of the business activity is

_____

Date _____

End Odometer _____ Stop Odometer _____

= _____

Destination _____

Tip: Use your cell phone to take a picture of the odometer, get an app for mileage tracking or use pen and paper.

For the ultimate guide to business from home tax savings, go to http://go.pillataxacademy.com. Select "Products" to get additional information about business from home tax savings.

Private business gatherings at an BFH are common and a "Business Guest Book" is required for tax deductibility. You'll want to capture the following information:

- Primary purpose of the event
- Date
- Who was in attendance?
- E-mail/contact information

Meeting minutes are another significant means of documentation. The following example is derived from a Word template that can be used for your business:

Business Team Meeting Template

[Click to select a date]   [Time]   [Location]

Meeting called by: _____

Type of meeting: _____

Facilitator: _____

Note taker: _____

Timekeeper: _____

Attendees:

1. _____

2. _____

Etc. _____

Please read:

_____

Please bring:

_____

Minutes

Agenda item: _____

Presenter: _____

Discussion: [Click here to enter text] Conclusions: [Click here to enter text]

Action items

1. _____
2. _____
Etc. _____

Person responsible: _____

Deadline: _____

Agenda item: _____

Presenter: _____

Discussion: [Click here to enter text] Conclusions: [Click here to enter text] Action items

1. _____
2. _____
Etc. _____

Person responsible: _____

Deadline: _____

Agenda item: _____

Presenter: _____

Discussion: [Click here to enter text] Conclusions: [Click here to enter text] Action items

1. _____

2. _____

Etc. _____

Person responsible: _____

Deadline: _____

Agenda item: _____

Presenter: _____

Discussion: [Click here to enter text] Conclusions: [Click here to enter text] Action items

1. _____

2. _____

Etc. _____

Person responsible: _____

Deadline: _____

Other Information

Observers: [Click here to enter text] Resources: [Click here to enter text] Special notes: [Click here to enter text]

It is good practice to assess your business annually. Create a plan for an annual business retreat that includes a calendar with daily and hourly tasks. Invite business associates and experts to train on topics that will increase your business's profits. One of the most important components of your documentation is the Annual Meeting Minutes. Below is a suggested template for your convenience:

ANNUAL MEETING MINUTES OF: (Company Name)

The annual meeting of (company name) was held on (date) at the location of (e.g. hotel), (city), (state)

The following members and/or managers were present at this annual meeting:

1. _____
2. _____
3. _____
4   via cellular device (e.g. Skype, Face Time)

The following other people were present at this annual meeting: None

1. (Name1) called the meeting to order at 3:00 p.m. After informal introductions, (Name 1) announced that she earned her certification in (coaching or any relevant information for notes) in (date)
2. (Name 2) was elected as the secretary of the meeting, and was the person memorializing these minutes.
3. The chairperson/CEO (Name) announced that the meeting was called by the members of (company) and determined that a quorum was present.
4. The minutes from the previous meeting were read by (Name 3) via his/her electronic device. It was noted

that the articles of incorporation could be viewed back at (company) headquarters.

5. The annual financial report from the previous year's end was presented that stated the treasurer of the corporation presented the treasurer's report, which stated that the previous taxable year (company), LLC had the following for the year ending 20XX:

a) A gross receipts total of _____

b) A gross profit total of _____

c) A net profit total of _____

1. Upon motion made and carried, the annual financial report was approved.

2. The wages for "Hiring your Children" were determined to be $9.00/hr. for (Name 3) and $11.33/hr. for (Name 2)

3. Upon motion made and carried by the members, the children's salaries were fixed at the following rates until another meeting or until increase in duties warrant an increase in pay as determined by the managing Vice President, (name) _____

4. Upon motion made and carried, the members decided that the next annual meeting shall be held on (date).

5. The following other items of business were conducted after (CEO name) opened discussion on increasing the company's bot- tom line:

- Brainstorming ideas to bring the company's bottom line from negative to positive
- Increasing flyer advertising

- Increasing Web presence
- Continuing the travel business
- Pointing more traffic to the (company) website
- Participating in/planning business "site surveys"
- Trying a couple of new business ventures for additional revenue
- Business 1
- Business 2
- Mall marketing; establish a partnership with an existing Kiosk owner to make sales and recruit talent for your business. Be intentional in following a parent company's marketing strategies for applicable products or services
- Three major marketing events hosted by (company) to heighten customer awareness of our products and services and to show appreciation for our customers' business
- Spring customer appreciation
- Fall customer appreciation park event
- Fall product sale at (e.g. hotel)
- (Name 3) discussed failed effort to expand into out-of-state market (name state)
- Campus marketing
- Strip mall marketing/ flyer, magazine or pamphlet distribution
- Request additional assistance from home base
- There being no further business to discuss, upon motion by (CEO name) and carried, the meeting was adjourned.

Dated _____

Member signatures:

1. _____

2. _____

3. _____

4. _____

Signature of meeting's secretary who documented this form:

_____

Date _____

TAX-SMART DOCUMENTATION Self-Coaching Questions

What is my biggest fear associated with my business taxes?

_____

_____

_____

Who are my tax strategist, mentor and professional?

_____

_____

_____

_____

How valuable is it to me to properly document my business to reap the deductions and savings legally available to my business? Why?

_____

_____

_____

_____

What steps am I willing to take in the next 1–3 days to become more business tax savvy?

_____

_____

_____

_____

Get Business From Home Tax Savings Tips:
https://www.taxhelponline.com

Chapter Nine

Income Techniques

There are ways to increase the bottom line that go beyond the profitable day-to-day operations in your business from home, some of which are outlined below.

LEVERAGED INCOME

Leveraged income is money generated for you from the work done by others. Some examples of leveraged income scenarios include:

- A business model that is franchised to other entrepreneurs (e.g. the ultimate leveraged income,

fast-food chains)
- Books and e-books sold through affiliates who promote these publications while feeding some of the profits back to the author
- A network marketer Who builds a sales organization from which they receive commissions on the sales made by independent entrepreneurs in their success-line
- A general contractor who makes a margin of profit on the work done by sub-contractors

PORTFOLIO INCOME

- Interest income paid on bank deposits
- Dividends from shareholding
- Profits from stocks or bonds

RESIDUAL INCOME

Residual income is revenue generated over time from work done one time. Some examples of residual income scenarios include:

- An insurance agent who gets commissions when customers annually renew their policies
- A network marketing or direct sales independent representative who receives income from customers when they reorder product every month
- An piano instructor who produces an instructional video for sale on the Internet
- A photographer who gets a royalty from an image every time it is downloaded from the photographer's website or authorized sales representative

- An entrepreneur who repurposes a printed workbook for sale in e-book format on the Internet

INCOME TECHNIQUES Self-Coaching Questions

What realistic income goal are you willing to set and work towards over the next year? $ _____

What percentage of your income will be a result of Leverage income? %

What percentage of your income will be a result of Portfolio income? %

What percentage of your income will be a result of Residual income? %

Please Help!

Complete the following sentence and e-mail it to: businessfoundationsuccess@tinafrizzell.com

As a result of using this book as a tool towards building a business foundation, I was able to:

Chapter Ten
Meditation

What is Meditation? According to *Webster*

Meditation is the act or process of spending time in quiet thought.

Benefits of meditation:

- Calming the body
- Lowering blood pressure
- Clearing a busy mind
- Creating a space for innovation

Meditation fosters not just inner peace but promotes thoughts and actions that can apply towards progress in your journey.

Aids in meditation:

- Walking
- Music
- Sounds of nature... like waterfalls, birds

When I ask my coaching clients how much time they have to meditate, I generally get answers like:

- 20 minutes
- half-an-hour
- an hour

There's no wrong answer. Most people say, "I don't have time" or "I don't know how."

Today you get a treasure. I'll walk you through a 3-5 minute meditation free of charge as a bonus for purchasing this workbook. Email meditatewithTina@tinafrizzell.com and request a date for meditation with Tina or a certified representative.

Listed below are a few FREE meditation apps for your enjoyment:

- End Anxiety
- Calm
- OMG I Can Meditate

Touch the App Store icon on your phone and select Search. Type in "meditation" and several free and paid options will be available. If you choose to download an app, you must provide your Apple password word for iPhone users.

MEDITATION Self-Coaching Questions

On a scale of 1–10 with 10 being the highest, how committed are you to indulging in a 3–5 minute meditation daily for one week?

_____

What can I identify as a quiet space for my meditation?

_____

To what date can I commit to adding a meditation app to my phone?

_____

TINA'S THANK YOU BONUSES

- One FREE 15-minute coach chemistry conversation ($Priceless value) with me or a certified associate coach with Just Traders International, LLC. Email me Freegroupcoaching@tinafrizzell.com

- One FREE 40-minute group tele-conference ($700 value) with you, a minimum of seven of your business partners and me or a certified associate. Email me at Freegroupcoaching@tinafrizzell.com

About the Author

Tina Frizzell-Jenkins is an executive leadership, business and empowerment coach. Her philosophy encourages the position of resisting the ordinary to do the extraordinary.

As a Coach, Tina managed the NASA, Goddard Space Flight Center (GSFC) coaching bench that has staffed 40+ internal and external coaches. Tina has worked with clients ranging from CEO's to executives to everyday individuals wanting to personally develop. She and her clients have tackled issues such as interpersonal effectiveness, tactical & effective leadership, effectively communicating, organizational change, work-life balance, strategic career moves, launching entrepreneur endeavors and getting results with teams. Tina has created and taught ICF approved training classes that earn coaches Continuing Educations Units

As an Engineer, Tina has been the program manager for large and small facilities projects nationally and overseas for the private sector and the U.S. government. The engineering journey was instrumental in helping her to get a good grasp on problem solving, customer service and managing expectations.

As a Business From Home owner, Tina enjoys hosting business development seminars and providing coaching and consulting services for entrepreneurs, professionals, and coaches driven to increase their influence, impact, and income. Tina is very generous and inclusive with sharing her knowledge and business tools with her clients.

Education:
- Honorary Doctorate of Humanity: Higher Learning Bible Institute
- Professional Certified Coach (PCC): International Coach Federation (ICF) trained at iPEC
- Leadership Certificate: Johns Hopkins University
- Bachelor of Science, Mechanical Engineering: Northeastern University
- Coaching Success:
- Coached an executive in staying on track with advancing his career while balancing other life priories.
- Coached clients in preparation for new jobs which were promotions that they competed for and won.
- Coached a client to have a positive shift in behavior

that caused management to acknowledge and applaud the behavior.
- Coached a business owner to overcome self-limiting beliefs, resulting in increased profits.

INVITE
DR. TINA FRIZZELL-JENKINS
TO SPEAK AT YOUR NEXT EVENT

Tina is available for half-day and full-day seminars. She'll speak or train at conferences and company events. Tina uses her educational knowledge, work expertise and life experiences to coach, educate and enlighten her audiences as they take aim at their goals.

For more information visit coachtinafj.com or email InviteCoachTinaFJ@tinafrizzell.com

Follow her:

CoachTinaFJ@facebook.com & CoachTinaFJ@instagram.com

Bonus Chapter

Intellectual Property: Your Hidden Treasure

Intellectual Properties are your hidden innovations. When you bring your innovations to life, you share your gifts for the world to experience or a smaller population of the world that you choose. Examples of these are screen-plays, books, music, websites, software, graphic arts, trade secrets, and medical procedures, to name a few. Your intellectual property could be your intangible hidden treasure. Once your treasure is unveiled it could lead to profits, self-satisfaction or both. You hold the key and the ability to create the map to unveil your precious "gems"... your intellectual properties. The question often asked is, "How do I uncover my treasure if my gems are not obvious to me?" The answer can be complex or simple. The complex solution is scrambling and figuring processes out on your own and the simpler answer is getting some context, some coaching and a few templates. First let's explore the context.

Webster defines intellectual property as a possession (as an idea, invention, or process) that derives from the work of the mind or intellect.

Intellectual property is such a big deal that federal and state governments had to get involved to keep order and ensure lawful conduct. The Government has patent, trademark and copyright laws that proscribe (forbid/prohibit; Webster's 1/27/16 word of the day) the stealing of intellectual property. In addition, preserving the safety of intellectual property is so lucrative that some law firms dedicate their entire practice to it.

To get a deeper understanding of a few types of intellectual property let's examine a few more definitions before considering some self-examining techniques that could assist you in unveiling your own gems.

Dictionary.law.com defines:

PATENT as an exclusive right to the benefits of an invention or improvement granted by the U.S. Patent Office, for a specific period of time, on the basis that it is novel (not previously known or described in a publication), "non-obvious" (a form which anyone in the field of expertise could identify), and useful. There are three types of patents: a) "utility patent" which includes a process, a machine (mechanism with moving parts), manufactured products, and compounds or mixtures (such as chemical formulas); b) "design patent" which is a new, original and ornamental design for a manufactured article; and c) "plant patent" which is a new variety of a cultivated asexually reproduced plant.

TRADEMARK as a distinctive design, picture, emblem, logo or wording (or combination) affixed to goods for sale to identify the manufacturer as the source of the product. Words that merely name the maker (but without particular lettering) or a generic name for the product are not trademarks. Trademarks may be registered with the U.S. Patent Office to prove use and ownership. Use of another's trademark (or one that is confusingly similar) is infringement and the basis for a lawsuit for damages for unfair competition and/or a petition for an injunction against the use of the infringing trademark.

COPYRIGHT as the exclusive right of the author or creator of a literary or artistic property (such as a book, movie or musical composition) to print, copy, sell, license, distribute, transform to another medium, translate, record or perform or otherwise use (or not use) and to give it to another by will. As soon as a work is created and is in a tangible form (such as writing or taping) the work automatically has federal copyright protection. On any distributed and/or published work a notice should be affixed stating the word copyright, copy or ©, with the name of the creator and the date of copyright (which is the year of first publication). The notice should be on the title page or the page immediately following and for graphic arts on a clearly visible or accessible place. A work should be registered with the U.S. Copyright Office by submitting a registration form and two copies of the work with a fee which a) establishes proof of earliest creation and publication, b) is required to file a lawsuit for infringement of copyright, c) if filed within three months of publication, establishes a right to attorneys' fees in an infringement suit. Copyrights cover the following: literary, musical and dramatic works, periodicals, maps, works of art (including models), art reproductions, sculptural works, technical drawings, photographs, prints (including labels), movies and other audiovisual works, computer programs, compilations of works and derivative works, and architectural drawings. Not subject to copyright are short phrases, titles, extemporaneous speeches or live unrecorded performances, common information, government publications, mere ideas, and seditious, obscene, libelous and fraudulent work. For any work created from 1978 to date, a copyright is good for the author's life, plus 50 years, with a few exceptions such as work "for hire" which is owned by the one commissioning the work for a period of 75 years from publication. After that it falls into the public domain. Many, but not all, countries recognize international copyrights under the Universal Copyright Convention, to which the United States is a party.

Now with a better understanding of the components that surround intellectual property it is possible to build your intellectual property foundation for your precious gem(s). To get started, I suggest picking your obvious gem that a community of folks will appreciate. If you know what gem you want to build upon go to step two in the sequence of steps below. Otherwise, examine yourself to determine what gem works best for you.

Start by considering an area where you are creative. For example, if you have a song on your heart, take the song from your heart and put it on paper. You can solicit someone to add lyrics to the words if necessary. Take the collaboration and get the copyright after completing steps 2 and 3 below. Go to www.copyright.gov to complete the legal documentation. Upon completing that process, you have legally made your song your intellectual property.

Even if your creative juices don't seem to be flowing, it is said that everyone has at least one book in him or her; therefore, if you don't have an artistic or creative ability that you can draw from, writing a book may be your quickest and best option. It's not as hard as it seems if you have the right coach and the drive. You can write about a topic that you are vastly familiar with or simply enjoy. The end result has more to do with your ability to research, connect with the right people and maintain the drive necessary to accomplish your goal of writing the book.

Consider using a coach to assist you with this process if you have difficulties or are just stumped. Email Tina at Bitesizebookwriting@tinafrizzell.com and I will assist you or give you a referral for another coach.

Perform the following steps:

- Recognize your gem.

- Polish your gem and make it shiny so that others will appreciate the value.

- Take the steps necessary to make your gem legally yours. Step two of this process is about polishing or perfecting the works of your mind or intellect. This is accomplished with some research. Investigation, experimentation and discovery are required to expand your knowledge base such that a community of folks will find value in your work. Once value is realized, then the community will want to read, listen to, appreciate, study or view your intellectual property in detail.

Third, take the steps required to secure your intellectual property in assuring that it isn't stolen or becomes the legal property of someone other than yourself. If your intellectual property is legally obtained, then the owner has all rights to the profits associated with the property. In most cases, obtaining the patent, trademark or copyright for your intellectual property will keep your property safely in your domain. It's smart to start securing your property before any public recognition is allowed.

Since we looked at the example of writing a book, let's go through the process of getting a copyright. The process starts at www.copyright.gov:

Select register a copyright Select log into eCO

Select new user, click to register

Complete the personal information to obtain login and password

Under copyright registration select register a new claim

Be ready to complete the application, make payment ($35.00 at the time of this writing) and upload your work

To begin, please answer the following questions about the work(s) you are registering, then click the "Start Registration." Your answers to these questions will determine the appropriate application for registering your work.

"Yes" to the questions below is generally the correct answer for those new to the copyright process.

Are you registering one work (one song, one poem, one illustration, etc.)? Check "No" to this question if the work is one of the following: a collection of works (such as: book of poetry, CD of songs and photographs), a collective work, website or database because these works do not qualify for the single form.

Are you the only author and owner of the work (or the agent

of the individual author who is also the only owner)?

Does the work you are sending contain material created only by this author? Check "No" to this question if the copy includes content or contributions by anyone else, even if the claim is limited to only the contribution by this author or the material has been licensed, permissioned or transferred to the claimant.

Select Continue Type of Work: Select literary work

Select confirmation box Select continue

Title of Work:

Does this Work appear in a larger work? Select No. Select Continue

Has this Work been published? Select No.

Year of completion—Type 2016 or the current year

Pre-registration number—leave blank unless you did a pre-registration

Author name:

Type name, citizenship and year of birth

Select all author contributions like text, artwork, and photographs

Type individual claimant (author) address Select Continue

Limitation of Claims:

Select Continue (if you are not using materials which have been previously registered)

Right and Permissions (gives permission for another party to allow others to use your work):

Type a name or skip Correspondent contact info:

Type person Copyright office can call if they have questions Select Continue

Main Certificate:

Type individual name (author) and contact information Select Continue

Special Handling:

Select Continue—unless you have a legal (litigation, customs, contract/publishing deadline) reason to rush application

Certification:

Select Certify Select Continue

Select Review/Select/Pay:

Select Credit card, after successful payment Select Continue to submit work

Select file:

Upload file (could take up to an hour to complete Select Complete submission box

New page designates the process is complete. The process is not complete unless this page indicates.

INTELLECTUAL PROPERTY Self-Coaching Questions (Writing a book)

What are three things that others have said that you do well?

1. _____

2. _____

3. _____

What are three things that you consider yourself an expert or fair to good at doing and or understanding?

1. _____

2. _____

3. _____

Observe the answers from questions 1 and 2. What are the similarities?

1. _____

2. _____

On a scale of 1-10, how important is it to YOU to document your intellectual property for yourself, your children's children or the world?

1   2   3   4   5   6   7   8   9   10

If you circled 6 or below perhaps consider purchasing a journal and writing/documenting your intellectual property for another time, or another season for someone you trust to take it to another level.

If you circled from 7–10:

What date do you commit to taking your first action of writing your first draft of the table of contents of seven to ten chapters? Or contacting a coach to assist you with the journey (coachtina@tinafrizzell.com)? _____

Resources

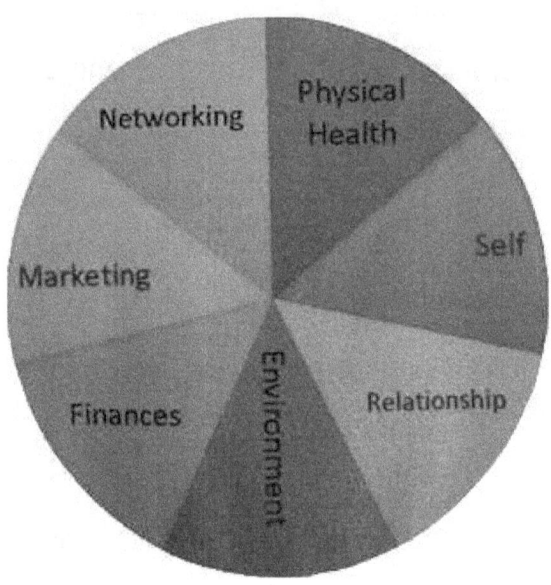

EMPOWERING BUSINESS EXPECTATION SEMINAR

Empowering Business Expectation examines the business owner's thoughts, goals, sales skills and vision as a starting point for creating strong business foundations. Join us as we empower entrepreneurs to create a vision on their journey to a strong business foundation that creates profits.

Business owners balance seven critical areas as they manage their business and lead their organization in customer satisfaction, innovation and increasing the bottom line.

Each participant creates a vision board as a visual reminder to maintain business balance while striving for success.

For more information visit www.businessfromhomeinstitute.com

Schedule a seminar for your business associates, email Coach Tina FJ: EmpoweringSeminars@tinafrizzell.com

READ UP JOT DOWN™ JOURNAL SERIES

R_{EADY} yourself to learn

E_{AGER} to absorb new information

A_{CCEPT} new challenges

D_{IGEST} and practice

U_{NLEASH} your P_{owerful} abilities

J_{UMP} at an opportunity to be insightful O_{PEN} yourself to the experience T_{RANSCRIBE} your thoughts to words

D_{EEP} understanding O_F W_{HO} you are in the N_{OW}

Journaling

readupjotdownjournal.com

THANK YOU FOR:

RESISTING THE ORDINARY TO DO THE EXTRAORDINARY!

Coach Tina Fj

www.ingramcontent.com/pod-product-compliance
Lightning Source LLC
Chambersburg PA
CBHW070648220526
45466CB00001B/342